THE NEW PR

21st Century Public Relations Strategies & Resources... To Reach Millions

Naresh Vissa

Naresh Vissa
THE NEW PR
21st Century Public Relations Strategies &
Resources… To Reach Millions

ISBN-13: 978-1535051552 (Krish Publishing)
ISBN-10: 1535051558

www.nareshvissa.com

TABLE OF CONTENTS

ABOUT THE AUTHOR

Naresh Vissa is the Founder & CEO of Krish Media & Marketing – a full service online and digital media and marketing consultancy and agency. He has worked with leading publishers, media firms and institutions such as CNN Radio, JP Morgan Chase, EverBank, The Institute for Energy Research, Houston Rockets, Houston Astros, the American Junior Golf Association, Agora Publishing, and Stansberry Research.

Vissa has started, shut down, taken over, quit, and sold businesses for his clients and himself. He is also the author of the #1 bestsellers PODCASTNOMICS: The Book Of Podcasting... To Make You Millions and FIFTY SHADES OF MARKETING: Whip Your Business Into Shape & Dominate Your Competition.

Born and raised in Houston, Texas, Vissa played a lot of chess and basketball, a few instruments, and fought his way to a First Degree Black Belt in Taekwondo. He graduated Magna Cum Laude from Syracuse University's Honors Program with degrees in broadcast journalism, finance and accounting. He earned a Master's Degree from Duke University's Fuqua School of Business.

USA Today, Yahoo!, Bloomberg, MSNBC, *Huffington Post*, Businessweek, *MSN Money*, *Business Insider*, *India Today*, *Hindustan Times* and other domestic and international media outlets have featured Vissa.

Subscribe to Naresh Vissa's FREE mailing list at www.nareshvissa.com.

You can contact Naresh Vissa at Naresh dot Vissa @ Gmail dot com.

THE NEW PR

21st Century Public Relations Strategies & Resources… To Reach Millions

Chapter 1:
WHY TRADITIONAL PR
IS A SCAM

I'm a publicist. I represent clients in the financial and economic space. I've worked with tens of clients over the years. And despite making a good amount of money from publicizing my clients, I'll be the first person to "out" most PR firms as scams. They're not what they used to be, largely because publicists still market their clients the same way they did before the Internet economy. They charge insane amounts of money, and they know very little about the term "return on investment."

When I was an undergraduate student at Syracuse University's S.I. Newhouse School of Public Communications – one of the best journalism schools in the country according to NewsPro – a few of my journalism professors would tell the crappy journalists to drop their major from journalism to PR.

"If you can't handle the pressure of deadlines, brainstorming, shooting, editing, writing, and putting together a good story, then don't do this. Do PR," I remember one of my professors saying.

For a one-day media tour (meaning the client has 15-20 minute interviews lined up over a 6-8 hour window), PR firms can charge upwards of $20,000. Their monthly retainers range from $700 all the way to $25,000 (depending on the quality and experience of the publicist or firm), with a three-month minimum. I'm not making these numbers up. I recently had to put together a spreadsheet of PR firms' rates for a client of mine, and these staggering figures are the latest industry standards.

Is the cost worth it even if your publicist can get you on as a guest on CNN or FOX News? That's a subjective question. To me, it's not worth it… because, given today's digital age, traditional PR generates very little return. Any PR strategy now has to consider the Internet.

Will the live video hit be available for broadcast and archive online? Will the live radio interview be available in podcast format after? Does the newspaper have an online digital version so you can share it on social media?

When is the last time you watched or heard an interview on TV or in your car's radio and you said, "This author is awesome. I can't wait to go home and buy his book!" Chances are, you'll forget the guest's name, product and website within five minutes.

Consider the case of Greg Smith – an ex-Goldman Sachs institutional salesman. He wrote a tell-all book about life on Wall Street, titled WHY I LEFT GOLDMAN SACHS: A Wall Street Story.

Smith got a big publisher, the Hachette Book Group, to publicize his book. *60 Minutes* and the *New York Times* covered it in-depth. Smith did interviews on all the major media outlets. He got all the publicity in the world.

Despite all the hoopla, Smith sold barely 20,000 copies of his book. He would've been lucky to make six-figures in royalties. Hachette didn't even break-even on their $1.5 million advance to Smith.

The Greg Smith scenario is what so many business owners and marketers fall for. It's why the PR and branding professions are still in business.

Every person I know who's hired a PR firm on retainer has been ripped off – even by the firms who charge a measly $700 per month retainer. There are countless message board threads and blog posts online of folks who felt duped.

People should do their own publicity work. I don't expect Donald Trump or Mark Cuban to be their own publicists, but someone on their marketing team should do it. They shouldn't have to outsource PR to a firm. That's why, in this book, I'll teach you *how* YOU can be your own publicist.

Chapter 2:
FOUR REASONS WHY PUBLICITY MAKES BUSINESS SENSE

1. Free

You don't have to pay anything to get media publicity, whereas you have to pay to advertise anything anywhere.

2. Believable

Ads can be hyperbolic. They can lie or be misleading, and most people who are qualified to be buyers are smart enough to know this.

PR paints a better sense of you. It's more real.

3. Multiplier effect

You can do a media interview, and that can lead to more media interviews if content producers like you or what you have to say.

If you're good enough for a national publication, then you're good enough for small publications and speaking gigs. There won't be a charge to you.

You can come out with a good ad, but nobody will run your ad for free. There is no compounding of advertisements, unless it's a video produced in such a way on YouTube that people start sharing it with each other.

4. Separation from competition

A civil engineer who is sourced by *Popular Science* isn't just another civil engineer. He's now THE civil engineer. Not because he's the smartest or the best... but because he was featured in *Popular Science*. And thanks to that feature, it'll be easier for the Science Channel and *Business Insider* to interview him too.

Chapter 3:
THE STATE OF EXPERT SOURCES

There's a large supply of expert sources. The problem is... most of these "expert" sources aren't high quality.

Media publications NEED high quality expert sources. There is a great demand for them.

Put simply: there is a large demand for GREAT expert sources. But there's an even LARGER supply of crappy experts. This supply of crappy experts far exceeds the demand for high quality experts.

So your challenge – as an entrepreneur, business owner or marketer – is to convince the media that you're a high quality expert. Media professionals look at the total package – not just your pitch, but also your background and accomplishments.

Chapter 4:
FOUR WAYS TO BUILD YOUR ONLINE AUTHORITY

I n the "new PR," experts need to build up their online presence. The first thing editors and producers will do is Google the name of the expert. They'll:

1. Visit your website.

Have a nice website that makes you look good. Include a section with all your media hits and mentions. Include another section that has your bio and another section with your books (if you have any). On the front page of your site, highlight that you have been featured by the media in big lettering (if you have been): "AS SEEN ON [CNN, FOX NEWS, etc.]" or "FEATURED IN [*NEW YORK TIMES*, *USA TODAY*, etc.]. This will build up your reputation and add to your media experience and credibility. The media likes experts who are familiar and comfortable with being in front of a microphone or camera.

2. Search Google News to see if other media have quoted or interviewed the expert.

One media hit will lead to another, which will lead to another and another. Being featured by the media should have a compounding effect. If members of the media can't find much on you through other media mentions, then they could write you off because you might be terrible in front of a microphone or camera.

If you have a popular full name like John Smith, James Johnson, Randy Miller, Brendan Jones, etc., then you MUST include a middle initial to distinguish yourself clearly on the Internet from the thousands of other people with your name. There's only one other Naresh Vissa in the world, so I don't need to worry about including a middle initial.

For instance, the actor Michael B. Jordan includes his middle initial to avoid confusion with the greatest basketball player of all time.

3. Check Amazon to see if the expert has any books, and if so, how many reviews.

If you haven't written a book yet, then definitely get on it. It establishes your expertise and gives the media a focused topic to discuss.

4. Look at social media clout.

The numbers of Facebook Likes and Twitter followers are key metrics with the media. Make sure you are active on all social media too (Instagram, Pinterest, LinkedIn, Myspace, Snapchat, etc.)!

Build up all of these and then leverage them in the pitch.

Chapter 5:
THREE RESOURCES TO GET MEDIA INTERVIEWS

To gain media presence, you have to start somewhere (small) with blogs and podcasts and work your way up to bigger media. It takes years… sometimes decades.

When I started out trying to get publicity, I represented myself because I had no money. I did not intend to spend $10,000-20,000 a month on a publicist.

I've gotten at least 50 media hits and mentions going all the way back to my college days. MSNBC, Bloomberg, *USA Today, Deseret News, Entrepreneur*, numerous podcasts and radio shows have featured me.

Here are some resources you can use to get cracking:

1. HARO (Help A Reporter Out)

HARO (Help A Reporter Out) is a platform that connects content producers (editors, producers, reporters, etc.) with sources. It sends out three e-mails a day – one in the early morning, one in the early afternoon, and one in the evening – with up to 50 queries *from journalists* (not publicists) who give an overview of the stories they're working on and the sources they need.

To get expert requests delivered straight to your e-mail inbox, you can join HARO at www.HelpAReporter.com completely free of charge. Once you start receiving the regular e-mail newsletter, seek niche queries that you qualify for. For example, if you see a query that is "Seeking Successful Entrepreneurs," then that's not very niche. There are hundreds of thousands of successful entrepreneurs around the world. If you respond to that query, then you'll be competing against the likes of Bill Gates and Oprah Winfrey. So don't even bother wasting your time by responding to those broad queries.

However, if you see a niche query you'd be a good fit for, then respond to it using the techniques I laid out on how to pitch the media. Let's say you're a private and independent stripper (so you only service parties, webcams – not clubs), and you find a query on HARO where a journalist is looking to interview a stripper… then you can respond back to the query with your pitch on who you are, and it will then be delivered to the journalist's inbox. Bill Gates and Oprah can't compete with that!

An hour after posting one query, the journalist can receive up to a hundred e-mails back from assistants, marketing assistants, publicists, and experts, so your pitch MUST stand out from the crowd using the recipe I lay out on pitching coming up.

I've gotten at least 50 media hits and mentions going all the way back to my college days, mostly due to my activity on HARO. MSNBC, Bloomberg, *USA Today, Deseret News, Entrepreneur*, numerous podcasts and radio shows: I've been around the circuit. I've read every e-mail and query HARO has sent for nearly ten years, and I haven't paid a dime for any of the publicity I've received.

2. RadioGuestList.com

Similar to HARO is Radio Guest List (www.RadioGuestList.com), except Radio Guest List sends one e-mail every two days or so, and each e-mail has only three or four queries. Furthermore, Radio Guest List only sends out radio and podcast queries. It's free to use.

3. iTunes

Doing podcast interviews that are published on iTunes is well worth your time. Here's why…

Podcasts will be on iTunes forever. They have a pass-along effect and long shelf life. A century from now, the mp3s will still be available for download. This is the greatness of podcasts on iTunes over terrestrial radio. Terrestrial radio shows air live and then disappear.

Think about all the people who own an iPhone or iPad or Mac… really any Apple product. And then realize that the "Podcasts" app automatically comes with all of these products.

The latest iOS updates integrate the Podcasts app natively onto Apple products. That means more than a billion people get the Podcasts app around the globe.

Does every Apple user use the "Podcasts" app? No. But iTunes has crossed more than a billion podcast downloads, and that number is growing rapidly. There are also now more than 200,000 podcasts on iTunes too. With so many podcasts come great opportunities for expert interviews.

Now, think about the types of people who own Apple products… we're talking about folks who have some tech savvy and money to spend.

The moment a user "Subscribes" to a podcast on iTunes, they have committed to receive all of a podcast's episodes indefinitely. This means they actually *want* to listen to every show. And it means this user is highly qualified. They're likely educated, working-class or studying, and have money to spend to improve themselves.

THIS IS THE ULTIMATE LEAD. NO OTHER MARKETING CHANNEL WILL PROVIDE HIGHER QUALITY LEADS.

In essence, Apple already does the filtering for podcasters. So, as a guest on a podcast, you'll be exposed to a very qualified audience.

Being a guest on a podcast with 1,000 listeners is equivalent to giving a speech to 1,000 attendees in a private auditorium. Consequently, it's not just hosts who stand to benefit from podcasting. Guests on podcasts have a great opportunity to sell themselves and their products too. Podcasts are always looking for good guests – thought leaders, authors, executives, and creative visionaries.

For authors, the podcast tour has replaced the book tour. It's no longer necessary to travel around the world to meet readers and autograph books. Authors can instead hold webinars or do a bunch of podcast interviews to get the word out and then forward folks to Amazon to buy their books… from their home and in their pajamas!

If you or your business has something of unique value to offer, then go to iTunes and search for podcasts you think you'd be a good guest on. To find podcasts to pitch yourself on, open the Podcasts app on your iOS device or the Podcasts section in iTunes, and search your expertise. If your niche is running, then type in "running" or "marathon training." If your niche is "stripping," then type in "stripping." See what pops up. If there are podcast shows in your niche, then contact those shows and pitch yourself. You can get the website of the show through its iTunes page. If it's not provided, then Google the show or the name of the host to find contact info.

Note: BlogTalkRadio is a competitor to iTunes and has many shows too. The quality of listeners and return on BlogTalkRadio is not as strong though. You can apply the same principles I laid out on getting iTunes podcast interviews to BlogTalkRadio.

Chapter 6:
FIVE STEPS TO PITCH THE MEDIA

There's no way you're getting publicity without trying. If you're a small business or start-up entrepreneur, you'll need to learn how to get in touch with media and get them to be interested in your story.

Here are some steps:

1. E-MAIL the editor/producer

More media professionals want to be e-mailed rather than called. Phone is disappearing as a way of doing business – for better or for worse.

I get annoyed when publicists or experts call me at random times of the day asking if I can book them for an interview on one of the podcasts or publications I manage.

E-mail your pitch. If you don't hear back, then follow-up a few days later.

2. Enticing subject line

The most important part of your e-mail pitch is your subject line. It's what gets people to open up your message. It needs to be a shocking, controversial, newsworthy or problem-solving hook.

3. Address the receiver

Make sure you call – by name – who your pitch is to. Include the person's first name. Don't send out a mass e-mail that says, "Dear Reporter,".

This adds a personal touch to your pitch. If you don't know the name of the person, then a, "Dear Reporter," or "Dear Producer," is OK. It's better than nothing.

4. Explain how you fit into the mission of the show or publication

If the medium you're pitching is about online dating, then start off by establishing yourself as an online dating expert. Include hyperlinks to your books, talk about your history – i.e. awards you've been given and accomplishments. On your website, you should have a media section that includes links to all your previous media interviews, so include the link to your media page so the content producer can see, listen or watch your established media presence.

5. Only at the end of the pitch do you "make the sale"

Include your contact information. Tell them you're available to discuss more.

In your e-mail signature at the bottom of your pitch, include your name, contact info, titles (with hyperlinks to any external websites like Amazon or your corporate site), and any other important info.

Why should contact info come at the end? Because most of the media will respond back to your e-mail if they're interested. Your contact info and "sale" aren't important elements to them. They know why you're contacting them in the first place.

Notice I said nothing about selling your product or service. It's only about selling your expertise and the quality of insight and analysis you can provide.

The last thing a content producer wants to do is run a free commercial for you or your business. That's boring and not newsworthy... unless you're a famous CEO of a reputable company or something in that league.

Chapter 7:
HOW TO WRITE AND SUBMIT A PRESS RELEASE

Consider submitting a press release for anything newsworthy.

As a business owner or marketer, your newsworthy stories could be:

- Raising a round of funding

- Appointing a big name to your management team or board of directors

- Launching a new product

- Reporting earnings

- Acquiring a new company

Taking the elements from your pitch, you can tie in the newsworthy parts into a proper press release format. The subject line can be your title. You can Google "press release template" to see what the format looks like and go off it. I'm also pasting a sample press release I did for a client at the end of this section so you can see the format in real-time.

To submit your press release to the wires without having to pay hundreds of dollars on a subscription, go to www.fiverr.com or www.upwork.com (formerly Elance/oDesk) and enter the search terms "Newswire" or "PR Newswire." Sort the results by rating, and hire someone with five-star reviews to submit your press release through the wires.

There are numerous press wires available – both free and paid – but Newswire services have the best connection to Google. They do a good job of getting your press release on Google News, leading to the release rising to the top of Google search. They also distribute your release to leading publications like the *Miami Herald*, *Boston Globe*, and *Digital Journal*.

Sample Press Release Format

[Full Date]

FOR IMMEDIATE RELEASE

[Enticing Title] (*similar to subject line of pitch*)

[City, State] – Leading Wall Street real estate note firm Watermark Trading Exchange (http://www.WatermarkExchange.com) [*hyperlink to your site and also write out the full URL because some wires will strip hyperlinks*] announced today that it has added the option for buyers to transact in bitcoin. Previously, users could only make purchases in U.S. dollars or euros.

Watermark Exchange will be the first trading company in United States to accept bitcoin for note sales.

"We understand bitcoin is becoming a very important way of paying for transactions, so we've been working hard to integrate bitcoin capabilities into our platform," Founder & CEO of Watermark Trading Exchange Val Sotir said. "Our team is constantly looking for ways to improve the trading experience of our clients. We really believe that adding bitcoin as a form of payment on our exchange will offer even more flexibility to our international real estate investors looking to add defaulted notes to their own portfolio."

Sotir, a 23-year Wall Street veteran in the trading and mortgage industry, said his firm has gotten numerous inquiries from international investors – particularly from Europe, South America and Asia – about being able to accept bitcoin. Watermark's entry into the digital currency space gives buyers more flexibility to pay.

Watermark has a designated trading desk to convert bitcoin payments directly into U.S. dollars, and it has retained BitPay as its payment processor. This move was meant to ensure Watermark could serve a larger section of the US investor market.

Bitcoin and digital currencies burst into the mainstream in 2013, and they have become a topic of great debate by politicians, regulators, retail owners, and financial professionals.

About Watermark Trading Exchange

Watermark Trading Exchange connects Wall Street institutional mortgage wholesalers with Main Street retail note buyers who are usually only able to obtain notes privately on a one-off basis. Watermark

Exchange is accommodating banks, larger hedge funds and private equity firms to sell their portfolios, creating liquidity so investors can buy more loans at much better pricing.

Watermark Trading Exchange has hundreds of assets for sale across the United States for investors to purchase.

For more information about the Watermark Trading Exchange, visit its official website at www.watermarkexchange.com.

For questions, comments or media inquiries, contact Val Sotir at [enter e-mail] or [enter phone].

Media Contact:

[enter full name]

[enter e-mail]

[enter phone]

###

Categories and keyword/tags: real estate, mortgage, notes, bonds, institutions, trading, Wall Street, finance, digital currency, investing, banking, investments, computer science, technology, education, economics, bitcoin

Chapter 8:
HOW TO HIRE A PUBLICIST IF YOU'RE TOO BUSY TO DO YOUR OWN PR

I f you have no time to do your own publicity, then what should you do?

Find independent publicists on www.upwork.com (formerly Elance/oDesk). Work out a tiered payment structure with a small PR firm (one or two person shop) so you **pay per booking**. If you struggle to find someone you like, then contact me at naresh dot vissa at Gmail dot com, and I'll connect you with an honest and small PR shop that can get you the visibility you need at the right prices.

Here's an example of a tiered structure:

Tier 1: top 50 ranking podcasts on iTunes, newsletter podcasts, newsletter interviews and features, pubs with dogmatic followings, mainstream media: like CNBC, FOX, CNN, etc.

Price: $150/booking

Tier 2: niche mainstream media: RT, Al Jazeera, CCTV, and relevant print pubs

Price: $100/booking

Tier 3: smaller online publications: TheStreet, big blogs, etc.

Price: $50/booking

Tier 4: small blogs and podcasts, BlogTalk Radio, terrestrial radio

Price: $40/booking

A tiered structure allows the PR firm to charge for performance (per booking), and the client knows exactly what he or she is getting and paying for. You both can decide the tiers and what criteria constitute each one. In this type of arrangement, the chances of anyone being scammed or shortchanged is near none.

Chapter 9:
FIVE WAYS TO DO MEDIA INTERVIEWS

Historically, reporters and interviewees have preferred to conduct face-to-face interviews. That is changing. Interviews can now be conducted via e-mail, phone, Skype, or Google Hangouts. Be ready to give interviews through all these media.

1. Skype

For video, radio, or podcast interviews, use Skype. The sound quality on Skype audio is much greater than landline or cell phone.

If the host of a show doesn't do Skype interviews, then that's a sign that the show has a small following and they're not running their production correctly. The sound quality of the show could be low, which means the production team doesn't know what it's doing. This is not a good way to conduct or run a business.

For audio interviews, use a good microphone. Here are some recommendations:

Mac users – Blue Microphone's Snowball USB and iRig… these microphones have some of the best sound quality on the market.

Cost: about $55

Windows users – Audio Technica… there are various versions of this mic. Generally, the more expensive the Audio Technica, the better the quality.

Cost: You can get a very high quality Audio Technica mic for less than $40.

USE A FOAM WINDSCREEN to capture and filter sound. Windscreens reduce the occurrence of wind, breath sounds and popping noises. They keep mics clean and extend their lifetimes. Most windscreens fit standard microphones.

Cost: $5

To buy equipment, USE AMAZON. Amazon is the one of the best online marketplaces on the Internet. The prices of products these days are INCREDIBLE… thanks to Amazon!

NOTE: DO NOT USE THE BUILT-IN MICROPHONE IN YOUR COMPUTER. Built-in mics are okay for casual use, but for professional quality, you'll want to invest in one of the microphones I mentioned.

2. Google Hangouts

Some up-and-coming, newer video shows will want to do interviews on Google Hangouts. Google Hangouts has even better functionalities than Skype. You can video chat with multiple users, insert computerized graphics, and record conversations.

All you need to use Google Hangouts is a Gmail account. You can use your computer's built-in microphone and camera because an external microphone or headset will be distracting to viewers.

3. Landline Telephone

If you're on a radio show or podcast that doesn't conduct Skype audio interviews, then your next option should be landline telephone. Landlines have better quality than cell phones.

4. Cell Phone

For print interviews with a newspaper, magazine, or blog, cell phone is OK.

5. E-mail

E-mail interviews are popular, but they benefit the reporter or writer more than the source because it takes a long time to draft a thorough e-mail with quality content. What you write in e-mail becomes your facts. You can't clarify whatever you say in the future.

Chapter 10:
HOW TO KEEP TRACK OF
MEDIA MENTIONS

W hat happens if the media or Internet sphere references you without your knowledge? First, that's a good sign. It means you're doing something right for the media to mention you or your work without your knowledge. You're getting free publicity without even trying!

The easiest way to track this is by creating Google Alerts for your name. Doing so is simple… go to www.google.com/alerts, and set an alert for your name or product in quotations. "Naresh Vissa" would be my alert. You can set as many alerts as you'd like. So if you're the marketing director of a company with several executives and quality brands or products, you can track all online buzz by creating Google Alerts for each item's name.

Chapter 11:
WHY GETTING ON WIKIPEDIA IS THE ULTIMATE PR STAMP

The end goal with getting all the media attention I laid out: getting a Wikipedia entry. But it's not so easy.

Wikipedia is now *the* go-to for research. Its search engine optimization (SEO) is one of the best – meaning Google usually ranks Wikipedia entries on the first page of a search query.

The WikiPolice consists of thousands of volunteers worldwide who monitor Wikipedia activity. If you try to publish a Wikipedia on yourself or your company, the WikiPolice will shut it down if it doesn't meet the Wikipedia standards.

There used to be a PR firm called Wiki-PR, which wrote Wikipedia entries for clients, but Wikipedia banned it for writing entries that weren't worthy enough.

My recommendation: get yourself as much PR as possible so that someone else (maybe even a WikiPolice member) can create a Wikipedia entry for you. Once you get your own Wikipedia page created, that's when you know you made it – for better or for worse.

RESOURCES

I laid out a lot of material in the book. It's impossible to remember everything. So I'll lay out the "smaller picture" resources you can use.

These resources are websites, apps, products and services to improve your PR efforts. They are not big picture tools like Facebook, Instagram, and WordPress. Those resources have entire chapters dedicated to them in my previous book FIFTY SHADES OF MARKETING: Whip Your Business Into Shape & Dominate Your Competition.

Hard PR

www.helpareporter.com – Become a source by getting expert requests from media and journalists delivered straight to your e-mail inbox.

www.RadioGuestList.com – Similar to Help A Reporter, Radio Guest List sends one e-mail every two days, and it only sends out radio and podcast queries.

www.google.com/alerts – Easiest way to track your online mentions in real-time.

MICROPHONES:

Mac users – Blue Microphone's Snowball USB and iRig

Windows users – Audio Technica

Syndication

Content:

- *Huffington Post*

- *Medium*

- LinkedIn

- Facebook status/Fan Page

- Publishers/blogs (big and small) in your niche

- Guest Post Articles (www.guestpostarticles.com) – marketplace that helps match guest bloggers, article writers, and marketers with blogs and website publishers who want guest posts, articles, and reviews

Podcasts:

- iTunes

- TuneIn (www.tunein.com)

- Stitcher (www.stitcher.com)

- SoundCloud (www.soundcloud.com)

- Player FM (www.player.fm)

- Spreaker (www.spreaker.com)

- Many other smaller distributors (you can get a full list by purchasing my previous book PODCASTNOMICS: The Book Of

Podcasting... To Make You Millions on Amazon)

eBooks (Amazon):

- KDP (Kindle)

- CreateSpace (Paperback)

- Audible (Audiobook)

- Smashwords (iBooks)

Slide decks – SlideShare (www.slideshare.com)

Videos – YouTube

Webinars – YouTube

Reviews – www.productsforreview.com allows marketers to get reviews of their products. For $10, submit a product for review, and the site will send your query out to a broad list of potential reviewers, who will contact you for a sample if they're interested.

Outsourcing Tasks (simple and basic PR, design/development, monotonous labor, skilled labor, etc.)

www.fiverr.com

www.upwork.com

Books

Surprisingly, there aren't many up-to-date PR handbooks that provide actionable guidance AND macro research on trends. Too many books focus on only one marketing channel (like just YouTube or just Facebook or just lead-generation) or spin their strategies into dreamy "get rich quick" schemes.

I've read (and written ;-) through the noise and found the best books that provide great roadmaps on digital marketing principles:

<u>TRACTION: How Any Startup Can Achieve Explosive Customer Growth</u> (2015 edition or later) by Gabriel Weinberg and Justin Mares

<u>THE NEW RULES OF MARKETING & PR: How to Use Social Media, Online Video, Mobile Applications, Blogs, News Releases, and Viral Marketing to Reach Buyers Directly</u> (2015 edition or later) by David Meerman Scott

<u>FIFTY SHADES OF MARKETING: Whip Your Business Into Shape & Dominate Your Competition</u> by Naresh Vissa

If you need any PR, online/digital marketing or project management services performed, then e-mail me at naresh dot Vissa at Gmail dot com and my firm, Krish Media & Marketing, should have solutions for you. I'm also glad to answer any questions you have to point you in the right direction.

STAY IN TOUCH

Tweet me @xnareshx.

Visit www.nareshvissa.com to subscribe to my FREE newsletter mailing list.

For a full list of services my marketing agency Krish Media & Marketing offers, visit www.krishmediamarketing.com.

If you have any questions or would like some online marketing or project management services, e-mail me at naresh dot vissa @ Gmail dot com.

Please leave a review of this book on Amazon!

REFERENCES

Berner, Maddy. "NewsPro Ranks Newhouse Top Journalism School in Nation." *The Daily Orange The Independent Student Newspaper of Syracuse New York NewsPro Ranks Newhouse Top Journalism School in Nation Comments.* N.p., 24 Dec. 2011.

"Get Everything You Need Starting at $5 - Fiverr." *Fiverr.com.*

"How to Find Radio Guests, Talk Show and Podcast Interview Guest Experts - Free!" *'Radio Guest List.com - How to Get Radio Interviews, Talk Show Expert Publicity and Podcast Guests!*

"Michael B. Jordan." *Wikipedia.* Wikimedia Foundation, n.d.

Roche, Julia La. "Greg Smith Just Got A $1.5 Million Advance For His Goldman Sachs Tell-All." *Business Insider.* Business Insider, Inc, 30 Mar. 2012.

Smith, Greg. *Why I Left Goldman Sachs: A Wall Street Story.* Print.

"Upwork, the World's Largest Online Workplace." *Upwork.*

Made in the USA
Middletown, DE
17 May 2022

65859878R00024